Don't Let Your Past Stand in the Way

Jacqueline Francis

World rights reserved. This book or any portion thereof may not be copied or reproduced in any form or manner whatever, except as provided by law, without the written permission of the publisher, except by a reviewer who may quote brief passages in a review.

The author assumes full responsibility for the accuracy of all facts and quotations as cited in this book. The opinions expressed in this book are the author's personal views and interpretations, and do not necessarily reflect those of the publisher.

This book is provided with the understanding that the publisher is not engaged in giving spiritual, legal, medical, or other professional advice. If authoritative advice is needed, the reader should seek the counsel of a competent professional.

Copyright © 2018 Jacqueline Francis
Copyright © 2018 Aspect Books
ISBN-13: 978-1-4796-0912-3 (Paperback)
Library of Congress Control Number: 2018900328

Table of Contents

Chapter 1: My Parents..................................1

Chapter 2: My School Years...........................9

Chapter 3: Adulthood.................................23

Chapter 4: My Sweetheart.............................41

Chapter 5: The Change................................50

Chapter 6: Closing Words.............................69

My Daily Prayer

Dear Lord,

    I just want to thank you for another day. Thank you for the lovely people you have sent in my life. Some have inspired me, stretched me, loved me and encouraged me. I love them so much. God bless them with all that they need in life.

    Every day is a gift from God, so I just want to say thank you Lord. As I walk the road today, may each moment be blessed with the brightness of God's glory, the goodness of His love, the beauty of His peace, and the presence of His hope. May His life shine forth in me from day to day.

    What I've learned throughout my walk with you, Lord is that the past cannot be changed. Everyone's journey is different. Life gets better when you are happy, and positive thoughts bring positive things into your life. Don't overthink. It will lead to sadness. Happiness is found within.

~ Amen.

Introduction

Dear Reader:

My Name is Jacqueline.

I would love for you to read a little about my life. You might wonder if I had issues throughout my life. Yes, I did. Life has been challenging for me. There have been some days when I did not know if I was going or coming. But I still persevered, and today, I try to live an exemplary life. But here is how it all began.

"Don't make promises when you are in joy. Don't reply when you are sad. Don't make decisions when you are angry. Think twice, act once, for you may regret decisions for a long time."

Chapter 1:
My Parents

My parents met each other in Kingston, Jamaica. Later on, they married and had five children together. When my parents were living together, my family life was very stable.

When we came home from school, we had a routine. My mom taught us from an early age to wash our socks and shorts. She gave each of us a basin for washing clothing. After we washed our clothing, we had to bathe. After we bathed, we had to sit to eat dinner. Then mom asked us about our day in school. We also had to read for her. At bedtime, mom would always pray with us. That was our routine after school. But Sundays were the best.

On Sundays, we had special breakfast. Cocoa or chocolate tea, duck bread (or hard dough bread), ackee and salt fish, steamed cabbage, callaloo, and nice things like that were prepared for us on Sunday mornings. Sunday was also the day that Mom baked cake and my dad bought ice cream. We all tried not to misbehave because if we did, we could not get the treat. These were nice times in my life that I can remember with fondness to this day. These happy times ended when my parents' marriage started to erode.

My dad had extra-marital relationships. This strained my mother's tolerance. When she decided to leave him, he became angry, which made it hard for her to leave. She did leave him but, despite her leaving, he would always come by and interfere with the way my mother was raising my siblings and myself.

She could not bear the toxic relationship anymore, so she left my siblings and myself in the custody of my father. This is how we ended up living with our father. I remember when my dad took me in. It was so devastating. I was so angry, but I didn't know how to express myself. I wanted to tell him that he should not take us away from our mother. I wanted to tell him that we needed our mother, but I was young and didn't know how to express my feelings to him. As a child, it was very confusing for me, having to leave my mother to live with my father and stepmother.

When we first started living with our father and stepmother, our mom would visit us when our dad was not there. She would bring groceries and other necessities for us, and I would long for her visits because I missed her. However, someone had informed our father that our mother was visiting us. As a result, my dad started asking us questions about my mother. When we told our mom that our dad was asking questions, she became fearful and she stopped visiting us.

It was not the best experience growing up with my father and my stepmother. I knew my father loved me, but his love was displayed in providing food, clothing, and shelter. The father's loving hug, the father's walk with his daughter, and the father's gentle talk with his daughter were not there. And his love, although I understood it, was no substitute for a mother's love. I don't think he knew how to express his love in any other way but providing for our needs. As parents, we might work so hard to provide material things for our family that we miss out on expressing our love to our children. Buying them things does not always meet their needs. They need your quality time, and to hear from your lips that you love them. When we keep saying that we are busy, then we'll never be free to spend more time with them. If we keep saying that we will do it tomorrow, then our tomorrow will never come.

Even though my father primarily showed his love in providing for our needs, sometimes, he also did special things that showed how much he cared for his children. When we all lived together, I remember my dad bringing ice cream and goodies home for us because he knew we liked it. If we were sleeping, he would wake us up and tell us, "Come and get your snack." He was fun.

I admired my dad. He was neat and carried a beautiful dimple with his smile. His smile was one in a million, with an open space between his top front teeth. But although he could charm the ladies, he could be, at times, very aggressive. One thing I must say about my dad is that if anyone tried to hurt any of his children, they would be in serious trouble.

What's more is that I did not appreciate some of my father's friends. When they came by our home, they would make remarks. One would say to my dad, "This one does not look like you. She looks like her mother", as if they knew my mother. In the back of my mind, I would think they had something against my mom, so I would speak to them with an attitude. I would give them dirty looks, roll my eyes and suck my teeth. It offended me that anyone would think badly of my mother.

"We make people cry who care for us. Those who never care for us, we cry after them. This is the truth. Once you realize this, it will never be too late to change."

To this day, I still respect my mother. She is a very kind and funny person. She is the type of mother that would play with her children. She is clean and neat. She is also an Adventist Christian. When my siblings and I were staying with her before my parents separated, she would take us to church.

I would always find myself outside of church playing marbles, flying kites or participating in whatever the boys were doing. Out of both of my parents, my mother was the punisher and she would scold me for playing when I should be in church. But after she punished, my mother would still show love, whether through playing with us, being affectionate or combing our hair. She was very fun-loving. She feared confrontation and did not like arguments, which made it easier for her to leave us.

I knew she left us with our dad because she was afraid of him, but I still wanted to be with her. Her absence really affected my life. Without a mother's guidance, being self-motivated and having high self-esteem did not come easy to me. Everything I would have learned from her as a woman traditionally, I learned later in life, which was a disadvantage for me. A mother would guide you into understanding puberty and personal hygiene. I did not know the value of childhood living, but I did learn the value of rain.

When I was a child, I used to love the rain. Why? It gave me the opportunity to let out my tears. I would feel so good while dancing in the rain and no one would know that I was crying, or see my tears fall down my face. It would make me feel weak to reveal my tears to anyone. I never liked when people questioned me because I did not like others knowing my personal business.

As I became older and mature, I understood that it is okay to let out my tears. I have also learned that crying is a form of therapy, and I can express myself through tears. When I see young people crying, I try not to ask too many questions. Sometimes it takes me back to my childhood. No one can truly understand another's tears. Mine is the pain I carried through my childhood.

When someone writes about their life or experiences, people want to know all the details about their life. Why? For many reasons. They want to know if it is a true story, or it might sound like their own personal story, and the list goes on and on. However, I feel very defensive when I am asked too many questions. "Why?" "How?" "What?" Sometimes, I just need a listening ear. So I ask that you grant me a listening ear.

But who was there to listen to me when I was a child? Whom could I trust?" For me, it wasn't easy to trust in anyone especially during my formative years.

Chapter 2:
My School Years

There are benefits to growing up in the neighborhood of Augustown, Jamaica. I learned street smarts so no one could take advantage of me easily, and that allowed me to stand up for myself. When I was in the 7th grade, my teacher had the nerve to hit me with a cane for not doing my homework. Corporal punishment is still allowed in Jamaica so this was acceptable. Yet, my father never would punish me this way, so I was very angry at the teacher. I was so angry that I slashed the teacher's tires. I was forced to write 1000 times that I was sorry. I did this quickly by taping two pencils together, and then I handed in the assignment to the principal.

"Are you sorry for what you have done?" he asked as he collected my assignment.

"No," I responded, "and if he hits me again, I will do it again".

At that age, standing up for myself meant taking my revenge swiftly but surely. When people spoke badly to me and put me down, I always got back at them. It didn't mean that their words did not sting, especially if it was an influential adult speaking about me. But I would get them back. I suppose I got that from my father. People could not mess with my father. And if they did, he would be sure to get them back. Besides, I am also loud and strong-willed like my father. Because of my mouth, many people were afraid to talk to me. The words I used were very vulgar. Often, I would curse like a sailor, and it did not take much for me to start a fight with someone. I would do anything to prove my point. One argument could go on for weeks, just so that I could prove my point.

With a temperament like this, you could see why it was hard for me to make friends. But it was easier for me to get along with boys. Perhaps my friends were boys because they also cursed like I did. Girls were too soft for me to befriend. I had a couple female friends who had a similar temperament to mine. I was the leader among my female friends. But with my male friends, I was equal, and we always found ourselves in places we should not have been, doing things we had no business doing. We were always picking mangoes, ackee and other fruits from neighbors' trees without permission. Even picking the school trees at times we should not.

I remember when I was thirteen years old and my teacher, Ms. Williams, called me into the staff office and told me that she needed to speak with my parents. Ms. Williams was my teacher the year before and was very used to my disrespectful behavior. I knew that if she wanted to speak to my parents, it was in regards to my behavior. But I asked, innocently, "For what?" and she looked at me like I was not important. Then she replied, "When they come, you will know". The next day I went to school normally, thinking that I would get away with the behavior, like I had before. I went to school and she asked, "Where are your parents?" So I looked at her the same way she looked at me the day before and I said, "They are home". She said to me, "Before this class is over, I am going to give you a letter to take home to your parents". I just walked away, not realizing how serious Ms. Williams was about ending my misbehavior this year, until the official envelope was in my hand. I could not wait to see what she wrote about me.

As soon as school ended, I opened the letter to see what it said. Ms. Williams wrote about the smart remarks that came out of my mouth and the countless amount of fighting encounters I had in class, especially with the girls. The letter also stated that if my parents did not show up the next day, I would not be able to go back to school.

Reader, you must understand that I had a good reason for fighting with the girls. In the schoolyard, there were some mango trees that grew and they bore a lot of mangoes. Sometimes mango would be the only thing I had to eat because I did not want to go home for lunch. Our class usually went out to lunch later than the other classes. So, the boys and I came up with a plan to go out in the morning before the other classes so that we could get our mangoes first. This would mean I missed part of the second class of the day. The girls in the class, who also wanted mango but did not go and get it themselves, would tell the teacher that I went outside to pick mangoes from the mango trees. This caused fights between myself and the girls of the class. Of course, the teacher was not pleased with my behavior, which is why she sent this letter to my parents.

I started thinking about what I was going to do about this letter. I did not want my father to know because he would share it with my stepmother. I did not want my stepmother to know because she and I did not have a good relationship. When my dad took me from my mom to live with him, my stepmother always had negative things to say about my mother and me. In response, I became very aggressive and disrespectful toward my stepmother. If my stepmother asked me to do any chore, she would have a hard time getting me to comply most of the time. If she tried to scold me, my dad would let her know that she could not scold me. There were negative feelings on both sides and I always tried not to ask her for too many favors.

I learned from a very young age to be independent. While I was still in school, I got a job at the local pharmacy. I used to restock the shelves, dust the items on the shelves and keep all the items organized. In return for my services, the owner of the pharmacy would reward me with little items like lotion, deodorant, shampoo, toothpaste, etc. Once in a while, I would get a small stipend of cash. So, I was used to taking care of myself. But the letter Ms. Williams gave me required the assistance of others.

I decided to go to my friend Vivine and to show her the letter. After school at her house, Vivine read the letter and looked at me with sympathy.

She asked "What are you going to do?"

I said to her, "Can you ask your big sister, Carol, if she could come to the school and pretend she is my big sister?"

It was hard for my friend to ask her sister for that favor because her big sister was like a mother figure to her, and she did not want to lie to her sister. So, I asked my friend if I could go inside to converse with her sister and she agreed. I went into the house, greeted the family and called Carol. We went outside and I showed her the letter. When she finished reading the letter she asked, "Where are your parents?" and I gave her some story because I was uncomfortable with her knowing I was not living with my mother.

I did not want anyone to know that I did not live with my mother. I would try not to have too many friends visit my house so no one would know about my family circumstances. I did not want anyone to have any criticism for my mother without knowing the real cause of her leaving us. I also did not want anyone to think badly of my father, even though it was his fault that we were left with him. I would delay going home from school in the evening because I did not want to be there. I was very embarrassed that my family was broken.

As a child, I would look at other families going on trips and having fun together and I would feel jealous because I did not have happy family trips with both my mother and father. I always tried to remember the times when I was younger and both of my parents lived together. I never wanted those memories to be erased from my mind. I kept the memories of better times alive by thinking about it repeatedly. Not living with my mother was shameful for me. I never revealed the truth about my family situation and I surely could not reveal the truth to my teacher, or even my best friend's sister.

Carol, without knowing the truth, went to see Ms. Williams, acting as if my parents sent her, my older sister, in their place. The teacher told her that I liked to fight and the words that came from my mouth were no good. She also informed her about my actions in class, such as me leaving the class, hanging out with boys, and fighting with girls. So, Carol listened to everything my teacher had to say. When we got to her house, she had an in-depth conversation with me regarding my behavior. I felt very sad because my mom was not able to do what Carol was doing for me, but not truly sorry about what I had done. I felt as if Carol had done something for me and I owed her. So, I tried to behave, but it did not last for a long time.

About one month later, on a Sunday morning, Vivine came to my house and told me that Carol would like to see me. I asked, "For what?" and she said, "I don't know". I got dressed and went with her to her house. On my way, I was thinking long and hard about what it could be that she wanted to speak to me about. What usually would be a ten-minute walk felt like an hour because I was so nervous. We finally got to her house. I went inside as if everything was alright but I was far from okay. I had breakfast with the family but the food had no taste to me because I was so angry; I just wanted her to tell me why she called me over to the house. While we were eating, she looked over and said to me "Jacqueline, are you okay?" and I asked, "Why do you ask that?", and then she said, "Your face looks unhappy". She was saying and seeing the truth, but I said "I am okay, I just have work to do at home".

She excused herself from the table and called me. We went outside and sat under the mango tree. The first thing she started asking me about were my parents. As she started asking questions about my parents, I felt nervous, anxious, and angry. I told her a false story about my parents to appease her. But I knew what was next.

She told me that one day she was going out shopping and she bumped into Ms. Williams. The teacher asked her, "How is Jacqueline doing? What's going on?" Carol answered, "I really don't know what the problem is." So, then Ms. Williams asked, "What are we going to do about Jacqueline?" The teacher continued, "She has a hard time getting along with the girls and has no respect." When Carol said this, I felt so bad but I still did not want to say what was happening with me at home. She asked "Why do you respond so badly when you are disciplined by your teacher?" As I heard the question, I felt so angry and rebellious because I felt it should be my parents correcting me and not the teacher. So, I told Carol, "The teacher is not my mother." Carol responded, "The teacher and I want to try and help you, but how are we going to do it?" My friend's sister reached over and gave me a big hug and these were her words to me, "You are a pretty girl and I would love to see you do your schoolwork. I am not going back to your school, so try and do your best and if you need help with anything just tell me". I said, "Thank you and I am going to try my best".

The good thing that came out of our conversation is that it made me calm down a little in school. That same teacher, Ms. Williams who used to reprimand me, became my mentor. Despite my rude behavior, she still had an interest in me. She showed me motherly love when I was not getting it. In response, I appreciated her interest and love. I worked harder to be polite to her. I was happy because she would always encourage me to do well. She invited me to her house on the weekends to help me with my homework and tutored me in the subjects in which I was failing. She noticed I was falling behind a lot and I tried to work hard to make up for all the work that I missed. She was very patient with me and would say words of encouragement to me. Even though I was promoted to another grade and Ms. Williams was no longer my teacher, she was still checking up on me, and she let me visit her home for assistance with my school work.

However, that did not last for a long, because Miss Williams' mother took her to the United States of America to live. Our good relationship only lasted for about three years. But, in that short amount of time, her presence in my life brought a major turn-around in my behavior, attitude, self-esteem and life outlook. Her departure was a big setback for me because I felt I was not loved by a lot of people. She showed me a lot of love and helped me, like a mother would do with her child. It was at this moment that I wished even more that I had my mother to guide me. Although it was not my mother's desire to leave my siblings and I, a part of me still blamed her absence for what had transpired throughout the school years of my life into my adulthood.

Ms. Williams was not the only teacher who was aware that I was falling behind in my school work. All my teachers knew. But not many were willing to help a rude, misbehaving, loud, stubborn, and vengeful girl like I was at that time. It was easier for them to leave me alone. When they tried to ask me questions, they could not get anything out of me. Ms. Williams was the only one willing to assist me even though I did not tell her what was going on in my home life. She must have figured it out. She purchased my school uniform and books for me. I remember the names of the books to this day. <u>New Junior English Revised</u> and <u>First Aid in English</u>. She took the time to teach me when no one else would and I will be forever grateful to her.

In spite of being rude to most of my teachers, I did get along with my gym teacher. I used to run in track and field and because I was a fast runner, I either started the relay races or ended them. One evening, I came home from school really late because I was training for the competition held during my school's sports days that year. I was so late in coming home that my father was home before me. Someone told him that I was on the street running up and down with the boys. When I got in, he was so mad that he spoke harshly to me. I didn't even get a chance to explain myself. The next morning when he was leaving, he warned me not to come home that late again. I told him that it was Sports Day, and he should come to see me but he said that he doesn't think that he'll have the time. To my surprise, when I was running, I heard the voice of my father cheering me on and I began to run a bit faster. After winning the race, I was looking for him. He saw me looking, waved to me and left. I'm assuming he went back to work. That same evening, I came home late. Astonishingly, he was as calm as a lamb. That night was the first time my dad gave me a hug and told me congratulations. He gave me permission to come home late as long as I was at practice for track and field. I knew what time my dad would come home, so that was around the time I decided to practice. I wanted him to see me practicing. It was a great feeling.

Unfortunately, running was not the only thing I needed to graduate from high school. After Ms. Williams left Jamaica, I relied on my friend's sister, Carol to help me with my homework. But she continued to question me about my parents, which frustrated me because I did not want to discuss the topic. So, I stopped going to her for help. I now had no one to depend on for assistance with schoolwork and I struggled immensely. When it was time for graduation, I barely made it.

Chapter 3: Adulthood

In High school, we were given the opportunity to choose an elective to study along with our regular classes. I chose sewing class. This prepared me for my first job after school. I worked in a factory by the name of Stylecraft Garment Industrial Factory. I liked sewing but working at the factory was not satisfying. For one thing, I was not allowed to sew a full garment. Different people were in charge of different parts of the garment. This job presented no challenge for me because I knew how to sew a full garment, and yet I only was trusted with one small part.

After that, I started saving so that I can go to beauty culture school, specifically Dornid's School of Beauty Culture. As soon as I accumulated the funds for school, I left my post at the factory without telling anyone. At that time, I was old enough to see my mother without having to inform my father or anyone else. My siblings and I would visit her. She helped purchase equipment I would need for my classes. She also contributed to the school fees.

I was very successful at that school and I graduated. I had a small beauty shop at my father's house. I truly loved working with hair and nails. However, health issues prevented me from continuing in the work I loved. Doctors advised me to stop working as a beautician.

I got a new job at a food industrial company, by the name of Grace Kennedy, and while working there, I had my first child. I worked there for a little while. Then, I was blessed with a city job with benefits in the University Hospital of the West Indies. God was always providing a job for me, but I was still doing whatever I wanted to do.

I believe that I am a strong-willed person, but others would say that I am stubborn, and my mouth is like a scorpion. When I graduated from High School, I felt as though I was grown and no one could regulate my words. I had no regard for anyone. I was an adult, and I was able say what I felt with no regrets or concerns. But I now had a child to consider. It made me realize that I had to change my childish ways to set an example for my young daughter. But my mouth was still a problem. I could not tolerate anyone talking negatively about me and not respond. I tried to change how I spoke around my daughter, but sometimes my words still stung.

As parents, sometimes we try to use the same method of how we were raised to raise our children. It does not always work, especially when you were not raised in a good environment. I was very protective of my daughter and I didn't want her to have the same upbringing that I had. I made up my mind, from the moment I gave birth, that no matter the situation, I would never abandon her. She wouldn't have to struggle the way I did and suffer verbal abuse at the hands of other people. I made it my goal for her to get an education, and to do well in school through encouragement and instilling in her the value of making education her priority.

This conviction that I had to show my daughter a good example showed up in many areas in my life. Before she was born, I partied a lot at dances, clubs, and other places. I used to hang out with boys. Even now, I have the tendency to hang out with men. But before the birth of my firstborn, I spent more time with guys. If we did not have money to go to the movies, we would be out late, sometimes until early morning, on the street corner playing music. But that part of my life slowed down when my daughter was born. Reader, I must note here that these guys were solely friends and nothing more. When I dated, my standards were higher than what I accepted from my guy friends. For example: I always dated educated men.

I started travelling to different places while working at Grace Kennedy. My first trip to the Cayman Islands was a disaster. The person who helped me to the Cayman Islands is someone I knew very well. I use to ask her on many occasions for information on how to work there like she did, but she would give me all sorts of excuses that made me believe she really did not want me to go to the Cayman Islands. This was ironic because if she needed anything done in Jamaica that she did not feel comfortable asking her family to do for her, she would ask me and I would willingly help her.

I'll never forget the Wednesday that she encouraged me to finally visit her in the Cayman Islands. In the midst of a phone conversation, she mentioned to me that I should look for an airplane ticket going to the Cayman Islands next week. I was so excited because I really wanted to travel to the Cayman Islands. The next morning after our conversation, I got up, went to the bank, got some money, and purchased an airline ticket. You couldn't find anyone happier than I was. I began making plans and arrangements to leave my daughter with a friend of mine.

The Friday afternoon when I got to the Cayman Islands, I was at the airport waiting for a long time. My friend knew my arrival time, since we had dialogued the day before the flight. I waited at the airport and was getting so nervous and anxious. When my friend came, she told me that the boss had an emergency and that's why she arrived late.

When we got to her residence and I looked around, I noticed packed suitcases, empty spaces and a bare refrigerator. I thought to myself, "This place looks like someone is packing to leave". Later that night, she told me that on Saturday, the next day, she would be going out. She also said that she had an emergency and she had to leave to go back to Jamaica that Sunday. After hearing this, I felt numb. I didn't know what I was going to do. I expected to stay with my friend in the Cayman Islands and for her to find a job for me. It felt like she was going to leave me here alone. I had to find someone to stay with in this new country.

So I asked her, "Could you ask one of your friends if I could stay with them?"

She said, "No! My friends don't know you. I could not ask them".

That night I could not sleep. My mind wandered over my situation. What was I going to do? Where was I going to stay? How could I make it here in the Cayman Islands?

The next morning, a lady came by to ask my friend for something and my friend told the lady that she did not have it anymore. I asked the lady if she was going to the supermarket to purchase what she needed and when she confirmed that she was, I asked her if I could come with her, and she agreed. My purpose for going with the lady was to ask her if I could stay with her and if she knew of any jobs I could take because I just came into the country. But I did not even have to ask her these questions.

While we were at the supermarket, I saw a young lady from my own hometown who I knew. Her pet name was Darling. I called out to her and we had a little dialogue. I told Darling that I had just come from Jamaica and the person I was presently staying with was leaving the country the next day. Darling had sympathy for me and invited me to stay with her, even though her place was very small. I told her that I didn't care about the size. I just thanked her for accommodating me. Darling came to see where I was staying so she could pick me up later that night, but I left with her immediately because I wanted to make sure that I was staying with her. Basically, it was Darling who paved the way for me to go back and forth from the Cayman Islands to Jamaica.

In my heart, I was angry with this friend whom I was supposed to stay with initially. I believe she willfully unaccommodated me. Years passed, and I saw the individual and asked her why she did that to me. She just smiled and said, "Let's not go there". I forgave her and we laughed and talked. Even at this time, we still keep in touch. When I speak to her, I seek to strengthen the banner of friendship where it was broken. May the love of Christ continue to bring us peace.

Although I traveled to other parts of the Caribbean, Canada and the United States, while leaving my daughter with a friend in Jamaica, I did not abandon her like I felt abandoned when I was a child. She would travel and stay with me or her father for vacation. I would also travel back to Jamaica occasionally to see her. We were constantly in contact with her. Her father and I would send clothes, money, or anything else that she would possibly need. In order to send her things she needed, I had to work. Sometimes it was necessary for me to travel for jobs.

It was a Monday morning when I went to the United States Embassy in Kingston, Jamaica. I got there at 4:00 AM and it was a long line. I thought I was not going to get a visa to travel to the United States because of the length of the line. At that time, I was working at the University hospital. So I had a good job reference written with a letterhead and I had a good bank statement. Those were the two main things I needed to show that I had ties to my country.

My bank statement was a mystery. My daughter attended St. Cecelia Prep School in New Kingston, Jamaica. For three consecutive months, I attempted to pay the school tuition and was told by the school's administration that the school fee was paid. I was the only one paying the school fee. Her father would send the money directly to me and then I would pay it. I assumed that her father was paying the school fee and still sending me the money so I did not question it. I just saved the money in my bank account. This made my bank statement look very good in the eyes of the embassy.

I had all the requirements for the interview. The shoes I was wearing were faux patent leather and they shone brightly. I finished my interview at 12 noon. They told me to come back at 3:00 PM. I knew when I heard this that I would be getting a visa. I was so happy. I felt like I could move mountains, even though I did not have the visa as yet. I walked back and forth to pass the time, and I showed up back at the embassy for 2:30 PM. I did not have to wait in line. I just showed the ticket with the appointed time and they told me which window to go to get my passport. When I got my passport, it said, "Indefinite Multiple", which meant that I had a visa that would let me leave the country anytime I wanted. I was so happy that I gave God thanks. I decided to go to the Canadian embassy that same afternoon. I prepared duplicate job letters and bank statements in advance. Just in case the United States embassy did not grant me a visa, I would then go to the Canadian embassy and apply for a visa. But I was so thrilled with my initial success that I attempted to try for a Canadian visa anyway. As I got to the Canadian embassy, the security guard would not allow me to go in, stating that they were not accepting anymore applicants. As I pleaded with the security guard, I noticed one of my classmates was working there as a security guard as well. I called out, "Hey Paul!" He looked around, saw me, came to the door and gave me a "bly" or a chance to apply. I was successful in getting a five year visa for Canada. I just could not contain myself. I could not wait to get home to call my sister. She was living in New York.

When I got home, my feet were so swollen that I could not take off my shoes. For the amount of walking and standing I did that day in my fake patent leather shoes, it was no wonder I could not take them off. I had to pour oil on my feet and cut the sides of the shoes to get them off. My feet were so tender. In spite of the tenderness and the pain I was feeling, I was still very happy and

I called my sister in Brooklyn, New York to share the news.

When I told her that I got a visa, she was more excited than I was. She said she was going to buy my plane ticket the next day so that I could visit her as soon as possible. So within the next two weeks, I waited for my daughter to finish school and start holiday. My daughter would normally go to the United States to see her dad on holiday because she had a visa before I got one. I spent 3 weeks in the United States and Canada because I was only allotted that amount of time off from my job.

It was so much fun meeting up with my sister, shopping, sightseeing, meeting my sister's friends and even helping my sister on her job. It was a very exciting trip. I decided to come back to America. Over the next 3-4 years, I used my vacation time to travel to Canada and the United States. For the first two years, I split my vacation time equally between the two countries. However, the United States became my main vacation spot , and I knew I would want to live there. After a few years of traveling to the United States, I made a decision to not go back to Jamaica. I was sure my daughter's father would sponsor her for the green card application process and I would not have to worry about her.

During my travels, I found out who paid three or four months of my daughter's school fee. It was an old friend of mine, Everton Williams. While his father was sponsoring him to travel to Canada from Jamaica, he was arrested by the police for possessing marijuana. In Jamaica, it is a minor crime. So he had to go to jail but only for a few days. When he was in jail, I used to visit him and bring dinner for him -- sometimes lunch. Fortunately, the crime was so minor that it did not keep him from eventually going to Canada.

During his first year in Canada, I heard from him a few times. If he knew of anyone travelling to the district where I lived, he would send a gift or token for me. The next year he came home to Jamaica to visit his mom because she was sick. She was admitted at the University Hospital where I was working at the time. Because of that, he asked me to 'give an eye' on his mom. Since the hospital was my workplace, I was able to visit his mom five out of seven days a week. A couple months later, he came back to Jamaica, because his mom's health was deteriorating. Because of what I did for his mom and him, he reached out and paid my daughter's school fee as a surprise, without any strings attached.

When I got my Canadian visa, I called him to let him know and he offered to purchase my ticket to come to Canada. I was blessed to have two people I could stay with in Canada: my friend and my sister's son. When I first travelled to Canada, I spent a couple days with each of them.

His mother did not live long after I went back to work, because of a stroke she had. She died within eighteen months. After that, he came down to Jamaica, buried his mom and returned to Canada. We still kept in touch. During my second visit to Canada, I spent some of my vacation with my sister's son and then with my friend, his wife, and his two children who were also living in Canada. About a year after, my friend got into a terrible car accident and passed away. I went to his funeral, but it took me a long time to overcome the grief because he was such a good friend.

After staying in the United States for over 6 months, I became an illegal resident, having broken the rules for my visa. The worse part was when my dad passed away. At this time, my mother was sponsoring me and I had access to an immigration lawyer. When I heard that my father passed, I called the lawyer, and told her the situation. She told me she could get a one-entry visa for me to go and come back. And she got it for me but I was unable to use it. My father's funeral was the day before my green card interview that would legalize my stay in the United States as well as my daughter's stay. I would not be able to go to the funeral on Sunday and make it back in time for a nine o'clock appointment the next day. I was not able to go back to Jamaica for my father's funeral and because of that, I was miserable with the world.

I used to babysit when I first came to the United States. It was a very stressful job because I did not know the laws here in America and the children I took care of could be very rude. I used to call my sister on her job and ask for advice. She would tell me not to scold the children because the parents of the children may have video cameras recording to see what is going on throughout the day. I listened to my sister but I was always seeking a different job. I just could not tolerate the nonsense. I could not understand the culture. In Jamaica, during the time I grew up, children listened to adults. But in America, the parents give their children too much freedom to disrespect them. I struggled with the two opposing realities.

The first babysitting job I got in America opened with a horrific experience. But no children were involved. My sister notified me of a babysitting job in Upstate New York, the last stop on the Metro-North. I was just happy to have a job, so I made the journey, even though it was so far that I did not go home until the weekend. The house was very big and included in my duties was housekeeping and babysitting. When it came time to wash the dishes, I used the dishwashing machine.

Now I had never used a dish washing machine before and I had no idea that you must use a special soap. The dishwashing machine was loaded with dishes and ready to go. I poured in the liquid dish soap that I would normally use when I washed dishes by hand, and I started the machine. Within no time, the kitchen was filled with bubbles.

It is a good thing that the babies were sleeping. I called my sister and she informed me that I was supposed to use a special soap. I found the soap and tried to open the dish washing machine. The dish washing machine would not open! My sister told me that it will not open until the machine is done washing the dishes. So, I hung up with my sister and I began wiping away suds and bubbles. They were everywhere! The machine would not stop producing the bubbles. I was so glad when the machine stopped. But I naively opened the machine and bubbles poured out. I spent most of that day cleaning up bubbles.

When the father of the babies came home, he asked, "Did you paint the kitchen?" I just smiled. I still have not revealed to the family what happened that day. The family was very nice to me, but I did not enjoy traveling so far to go home on the weekends. I got lost the first week, when I was coming back home. Because of the distance, I sought another position.

I found one in the city. It was not the most pleasant experience. The mother of the children was like a slave driver. The new position made me wish for my first job, regardless of the distance. She and I could not see eye to eye because of my temperament and my mouth. So, one Friday, she paid me and fired me.

Fortunately, there was another babysitting job waiting for me.

Dealing with traveling, tireless bosses and rude children was part of babysitting, but I stuck with it because I wanted to provide for my daughter. As soon as I got my green card, I applied for other jobs. I was glad to leave babysitting behind.

Chapter 4:
My Sweetheart

Eventually, my daughter officially came to live with me in the U.S. Then, I started dating the person who would become my husband. When I met my husband, who was also named Everton, he was staying with one of his family members that I have always called 'Grandma'. It was a Sunday morning and I was taking a little girl over to the house. I saw him having breakfast. I said, "Good Morning. Can you share your breakfast?" And of course, with a beautiful smile, he said, "Yes". And that was the end to the conversation. I left, thinking nothing of the meeting.

A couple days after, I was in the neighborhood and Everton saw me. He came over and said, "Hi. You are in my neighborhood", with a blush on his face. He asked to get my contact information and we exchanged telephone numbers that day. He called two days after and we conversed. For two months, we continued to talk over the phone. He then asked me if he could take me out to a movie on a Sunday afternoon. I agreed. But when he came to pick me up for the date, he was wearing full white and I cheekily asked him, "Are you going to play cricket?" We did not go out that day but we stayed in and talked. He set up another date and he was sure to wear appropriate attire. We went to the movie and he was so soft-spoken, so gentle, so loving.

Unfortunately, I was dating someone else at the time but Everton was satisfied with just being friends. I told my sister Dell about him and she wanted to meet him. I introduced them and she fell in love with him. Even to this day, everyone in my family likes my husband. You would think he is the blood relative and I am the in-law. After first meeting him, my sister Dell encouraged me to give him a chance. I took her advice. I gave up the relationship I was in to pursue a relationship with Everton. And to this day, I have not regretted that decision.

Everton and I have always respected each other and listened to each other. Everton is a great husband. I admire the qualities that my husband has. He is always encouraging me. He never lets me feel less than myself. He is honest and quiet. He takes his marriage and his family life seriously. He adores me. He does everything to make me feel happy as a wife. But he hates when I am in conflict and when I am loud. It can kill his spirit when I get loud and boisterous. When we do have misunderstandings, he never goes to bed without my hug and my kiss. He always says, "I love you J. Have a good night." I love these qualities about him and love the way he has treated my first daughter.

My daughter has a good relationship with him. He treated her as if she was his own child. He picked up the responsibility of helping her with anything that she needed in her education. After we got married and had our second child, my life was completely different.

Although my first daughter had a stepfather in her life, her biological father would also express the importance of making sure her education came first and giving it her all. Especially, since her father had a higher education than I did. We both reinforced that her schooling was the path to success.

When I see my daughters' fathers interact with them, it makes me feel wonderful because I did not get that when I was young. When I see how their fathers treat them, it is like I am getting the love through their interactions. Like I said, my father did not tenderly care for us, so it makes me feel happy to see my children experience it. Also, my husband shows me the care that I felt deprived of when I was a child. I have come full circle.

As a mother, I try to have conversations with my children. I try to ask them questions. I might not get the true answer, but I still ask questions. As a mother one of the things I hate the most is when I ask my children a question, and they lie to me. It makes me feel like they are burying me alive. It really hurts me to know that my children do not trust me with the truth, but I have to remember that the bible tells parents not to provoke their children to wrath. So I try not to get too angry with them. But I always say to them, "Tom drunk, but Tom is not a fool", so they know that I don't believe them.

I want my children to benefit from my experience. Specifically, I ask my children if they are dating because the person you date can become the person you marry. The person you marry can change your life for better or for worse.

Dating is when you are getting to know someone, and much must be considered when you are choosing your future mate. This is the time when you look for red flags. For example, if the person you are dating is lazy before marriage, they will be lazy after marriage. It is during this time that you find out if someone is abusive. Fortunately, I have never been in an abusive relationship so I can only advise my children to not stay in one. If you date properly, this stage would reveal problems you might have if you marry. You must be very attentive during the dating stage.

There is a lot of advice I give my daughters that stems from my childhood experiences. As a mother, I make sure that I tell my daughters that if they are dating someone with a child, you cannot love the man and not love his child or children. When I was a child I felt unloved by my stepmother and I would not want any other child to feel the way I felt.

I was shocked to know that my husband and I were recognized as a couple that many look up to in my church. I have been asked a couple of questions about marriage. One question that was asked to me was, "How do you deal with marital problems when they come along?" My answer is that in every marriage, there are ups and downs. Even in my marriage. Couples need to remember that there should always be respect, you should always give a listening ear and be careful of the words used toward your spouse. I remind my daughters of this as well.

If you are married and your marriage is in trouble, be careful who you go to for counseling. It is possible that you are receiving counsel from someone who is divorced, and rebellious about what they ought to do in a relationship, and they may advise you based on their bad experiences. Sometimes they would advise as to how they would handle the situation, which may not be wise since they are divorced. I tell my daughters these things.

I ask them about dating and marriage and respond to their answers the best way I know. My mother never had conversations like this with me. But I make sure that I have these conversations with my children, even though they might feel pressured by me. I tell my children to avoid sharing sensitive information with someone they are dating, avoid getting too attached or getting intimately involved, and avoid being alone with the person they are dating. But most of all, I want them to know that I am there for them.

Today's dating is different from dating in the past, especially for a Christian. Promiscuity is more acceptable now than ever before. But I want my daughters to approach dating with much care and prayer. I want my daughters to stand firm in what they know to be true. So far, they have stood up and I am proud of them.

One of the best birthdays I had with my children was five years ago. It was just the five of us: Myself, my husband, my daughters and my granddaughter. What made it so special was my first born telling me that she and her sister wanted to talk to me without any argument from me. So I gave them their request. They told me what they didn't like about me, and what they did like. It was good for me as a mother and a wife to hear my family's concerns. I gave them my words to be a better mother and wife to my family. I know it must have been hard for my children to say these things to me. They got a big surprise from me. They thought I was going to fuss with them and say, "How dare you say these things to me!" However, I do not believe that because I am the parent I should not humble myself. I want my children to know that not only am I their mother, I am their friend. When it is time for me to put my foot down as a mother, I will do so. I want my children to know that I have their back and they can come to me with any problem they are facing. But, at the same time, I have to tell them when they are wrong. As a mother, you must not give up on your children. I always want my husband, children and my granddaughter to know that I love them.

My youngest daughter is currently in college and the oldest one has graduated with her baccalaureate degree in Accounting. Now with both of my daughters having followed the guidelines set out for them, we, as parents, are proud of their academic achievements.

Chapter 5:
The Change

When I came to the United States, I reconnected with my mother. Our relationship has grown stronger but, at first, it was not easy. I had so many things I wanted to get off my chest.

I told her, "As a mother, I believe you could have done more, for my siblings and me, even though it was not your will to leave us." But she responded with different excuses. I didn't believe her excuses because they did not seem like the truth to me.

After hearing what my mom had to say to me, I replied back and said, "As a mother, it's your responsibility to take care of your children".

When conversations like this came up, they never really ended on a good note. One thing I did not do was disrespect my mother. I made it my duty to call her every day. My family and I would visit her from time to time. Despite the abandonment and all that I endured, I still love her. Sometimes she would wish that she could turn back time. Although it's too late and the damage is done, it's still a pleasure and a wonderful feeling to know that I have a mother.

When I moved to the United States without a green card, it was my mother that helped me obtain one, which I appreciated, so very much. Deep down inside, I still feel that taking care of me while I resided in Jamaica and making sure I was happy was more important than my green card. There are times when we have good conversations on the phone and other times in which conversation can be pointless. Sometimes when I have problems, I can call my mother and she will give some good advice to me.

Now that she is older, I am her right-hand man. I pray each day for my mother that she would have peace and comfort within herself. I pray that she would not sit and wait for her children to reach out to her but would reach out to them first. She needs to show her children love and appreciation.

As for my stepmother, my relationship with her was very bitter. I have found the Lord and I have been reading his word more. It has taught me how to let go of hatred, animosity, backbiting and evilness. I knew I had these negative feelings inside of me towards my stepmother. I would talk to her with disrespect because these negative feelings would bubble up whenever I was around her. I am glad that I have reached a stage in my life where we both can make amends. I can call her and she can call me. We can sit at each other's dining table. We can give each other good compliments. We can embrace each other without any hard feelings. I just want to say to you readers that I have overcome my hatred.

At this point I don't know who to call my enemies because I have made peace with all those who may have been enemies at some point in my life. People might say I am their enemy, but they are carrying a big burden and they are so unhappy. I know because I was doing that same thing. I was holding grudges, keeping malice, being vindictive and those are heavy loads to carry. But now I am free from my burden. I have asked for my "70 times 7" forgiveness from

"God is love. True love is putting yourself last and others first. Love must be sincere, not selfish or unforgiving. You must denounce evil and love your enemies."

family, friends and associates. Those who forgave me I accept, and those who did not forgive me – well, that's alright with me. They have the 'pain', not me. I am happy. I am free.

Before I became a Christian, I was not an easy person to deal with. If someone tried to hurt me I would return the favor. The words from my lips and tongue were like the sting of a wasp and those who could not take it would cry and complain. Others would sting back or they would be mad at me for a while.

Even though some conflict would exist in my relationships, I was a compassionate person and was willing to give a helping hand where necessary. I started attending church when I was 30 years old but those who know me would say that there was no real change in me.

It was not until I turned 40 that I started taking God seriously and reading the Bible. I realized that it made a difference. I started noticing some changes in my life, where if I thought I hurt someone or if someone brought it to my attention that I hurt him or her, I was willing to apologize. I became a true Christian and realized I was accepting the new me. Based on this new-found joy, conflicts and misunderstandings were quickly cleared up and things would return to normal faster than before. I am trying to build a stronger relationship with the Lord, and in doing so, my family devotions and Bible studies have expanded my knowledge of the Lord more and more each day.

This change in me did not come suddenly. It was a process. I grew into this person I am now. I just got to a stage where I grew numb to negative feelings. When the negative feelings come, I expect it. When the positive feelings come, I thank God. I want my family and friends to realize how much I am trying to get closer drawn to God's words, so that others can see that in me.

At all times, not sometimes, I should remember the love of Jesus. God hates when we sin, but he loves all sinners, including myself, who sins every day. My family, relatives and friends may not know how much I pray for them, asking God to keep them safe. Now that I am older, I understand if I hold onto grudges and animosity, it will destroy the unity between family members and friends. I was motivated to put my thoughts into writing and to let my family and friends know how much I care for them and love them.

While I have mourned the passing of many family members, I have grieved the most over 3 particular deaths: my father, second eldest brother and oldest sister.

Regretfully, my father passed away before any one of us had the opportunity to send for him and care for him in the United States. We thought he would get better, but he didn't. His death affected me so badly that I was miserable toward everyone, including my siblings.

Despite the natural rivalry between siblings, we had love. We may not have known how to express it but I would love for their children to know that I will always love them.

What is hard for me to understand is how distant we have become as siblings. When we were all in Jamaica, we used to have each other's back. Whoever came up first to the U.S. would send things down for us. Also, when they came down, we would all get things from them for ourselves and for our children. Now everyone is in the U.S. So I do not understand why we are so distant.

Before my second-eldest brother and oldest sister passed, they both made the same request of me: stand by their children. I gave my word to do just that. However, I feel that now their children are adults and have their own lives. Our relationship is strained due to our busy schedules. I still place great emphasis on love and forgiveness.

I can see where God has blessed me with health and life. Therefore, I try so hard as a Christian to stay away from negativity and make the choice to de-escalate situations by letting the other person say their peace without being challenged.

Since I have turned 50, life has become more valuable and serious. I decided to re-dedicate my life to Christ on my 50th birthday, and it was a wonderful feeling because of what I've learned throughout my years. The different experiences, both positive and negative, have made me look back and create a line distinguishing my past from now. No more negative criticism. I still find myself dealing with a lot of challenges. But if the fingers are pointed at me, I will take the blame in order to have a peaceful life. However, this is only with my family!

The reason for this is because someone must make the step to make peace and ensure that the family is still bonded. And I must say my husband always emphasizes the importance of family; he hated hearing me fuss with my family. He always tries not to get involved in disputes. But as soon as the dispute is over, he will speak to me about it. His voice is always soft and persuades me to listen and talk to him. He always encourages me to see the bigger picture and not to focus on the issues that we will soon get over in a day or two. He would remind me of his relationship with his siblings and how powerful that relationship can be. He uses his family to show me that the things my siblings and I fuss over are nothing in comparison to the wonderful relationship that can flourish.

Keep your heart open with good thoughts. Hold your head up high. Your blessings are on the way. Never explain yourself to anyone. The person who does not like you will not believe it.

It's time for me to move on from the pain that I am carrying. Although I changed my life around for the better, some people from the past try to stop my growth and happiness because they won't allow my past to remain my past. Sometimes it seems as if they are judging me by my past actions. One thing I tell myself is that life doesn't come with any guarantees but it is filled with possibilities and challenges. Along my journey through life, I know hardships will come my way. So, I must have an open mind for new ideas and a good heart for forgiving others. This is how I move on.

Somedays I am so angry and I feel out of control because of how people judge me. People judge me by the way I live without knowing what I am going through. Now that I am more mature in my Christian journey, I am more willing to be there when someone needs to talk and not be quick to judge. We are all humans and we make mistakes. When tempted to judge, just think for a minute about how Jesus would think of us. Walk with him and talk to him. I know He will listen. You can have faith in Him. He will never let you down. For we must pray and ask him for guidance, it is important. When you love the Lord, you must remember how to speak, act, and think differently because you are within him.

Sometimes, in my quiet time, I think about what the future holds for me. But God already knows my future, so I leave it to him. As a child, seeing other children grow up with their parents made me feel jealous, but now that I am older and have my own family; I no longer feel that way. Jealousy can become a big problem in our lives. When we are jealous of others, it can ruin our relationships. God has blessed me with so much and I am so thankful that there is space for jealousy.

I should not give priority to someone who does not place me as a priority in their life. When relationships are balanced on a scale, they work best.

We all need mercy from God, family and friends. Sometimes we beg and plead for it. We want mercy and grace from God for ourselves, but we are not willing to give mercy to others. God wants us to show love and compassion to others who are mean and hateful to us. When we do good things, it shows a good picture of God's love to others. I used to criticize others and not have compassion because the love of Christ was not in me. Now, I have the power of His love to shine in me. I do not deserve his love, but because of God's love for me, he gives grace and mercy. Now, because I realize grace has been given to me, I judge less and show more compassion.

We all point fingers at each other, calling out the hypocrites. But we are all hypocrites. Some people play the game so well but when their true colors start to show, it can be surprising. None of us are perfect, but if we try to convince others that we are perfect, then we are hypocrites. Be careful of self-righteous people.

As an adult, I am very cautious in my associations with people. It's very easy to criticize and judge our neighbor for their mistakes. We tend to justify our wrongs but we are quick to criticize others. When we surrender our lives to God, we come to the realization that we do not have all the answers. As we spend more time with Jesus we find that He is the answer.

Sometimes it is hard to ask people for help. As Christians, we say we have love for one another. Yet we let everyone know that we have helped someone for purely selfish reasons. Sometimes we let people know that we have helped someone after the person we have helped stops speaking to us. Or maybe we want the person we have helped to feel some obligation to us. Or maybe we want to look good in the eyes of others. I don't like when people have the upper hand over me. So, because of that I keep my hardships and my pain to myself. I thank God for his loving words which give me peace of mind so I don't let those hardships, my pain, and the negativity in life hold me down or hold me back.

Sometimes negative thoughts enter my mind. When I encounter these thoughts, this is when I spend my time in prayer with Jesus. When negative thoughts come to you, the best bet for you would be to spend time with Christ. Take the time to read his word and allow Him to come into your heart and speak to you. We would be greater in our lives if we invited him to spend time wherever we are.

In His word, there is a solid foundation that God has provided for our personal growth. Focusing on God's word gives me inspiration that

I feel in my heart. If I focus on God, I will develop a solid love for his word.

Life doesn't allow for us to go back and fix what we have done wrong in the past, but it does allow for us to live each day better than our last. I can smile through the pain, and my tears. I can praise the Lord through times of trouble and take comfort in the knowledge that, as a Christian, what I'm going through isn't the end. No matter what kind of bad day I have, I should still lift Jesus up first.

Lord, I'm stepping out in faith trusting that today will be a better day than yesterday, Amen.

Sometimes when I think my prayers are not answered, I often wonder if it is because I have not truly forgiven someone in my heart. All we need to do is give our pain to Jesus, then leave it in God's hands and be free. When you have wronged someone, ask for forgiveness. When someone has wronged you, ask God to put forgiveness in your heart. Yes, even if that person hasn't said sorry. Don't stop there. Start praying for the person who wronged you. Ask God to put more love in your heart for them. You will find it difficult to have love toward someone who has wronged you but you can do it. It might look impossible but Philippians 4:13 says, "I can do all things through Christ which strengtheneth me." (KJV) Ask God to remove all hatred and bitterness from your heart and replace it with his sweet forgiveness.

Time is short, for no one is promised tomorrow. So live right today. Whatever or whoever is standing between you and God, surrender it today. For there is no sin too big for God to forgive, and nothing is worth missing out on everlasting life with Jesus. Take time to smell the roses - actually smell the roses - God created them for us to enjoy. Love yourself. God wants you to be happy. So enjoy life with family, friends, and loved ones, no matter how badly you've messed up or how awful you feel about yourself. I wish my family and friends could see that we could all enjoy life together. Give all that pain to Jesus and allow him to wash it all away forever.

A couple of months ago, I did a survey on myself to see how others viewed me, and I was very happy I did it. Some people wonder why I did it. I wanted to know how people see me and what they think of me before I die. I go to a lot of funerals and hear people say all kinds of nice words about the dead. But when the person was alive they didn't get those warm, loving words. You could be sick and no one calls. Sometimes it feels like you are the only one reaching out. It is good to tell someone that you care for them when they are alive. Give them a call. Give them roses when they are alive so that they can smell them. All the things that are said about the dead have no meaning because the dead cannot hear. I was extremely happy to hear the feedback on my survey. I was happy not only to hear it, but to make improvements in my life based on the feedback.

For my bad habits that I am trying to break, I need the Holy Spirit to give me the strength to get through it. Jesus is the only answer if we want to break bad habits.

Sometimes, as we journey in life we lose things. Some can be replaced, and some cannot. The most important thing to remember is that the source of everything is God in our lives.

Sometimes I wonder if Christ would come now, would my name be called to enter into the kingdom? I know that I need to love in order to enter the kingdom. We call ourselves children of God and family of the father but we are still far from having love for one another. The Bible tells us in so many ways about love.

Some may wonder why the topic of love is so heavily discussed. After growing up without love in my life and finally receiving it from my husband, my children, and God, I now see its importance, and I am appreciative of it. It is important to have love in your life and to share it with those who do not have it.

Before I knew Christ, I did not have love. When you do not have love, you will not understand what love is. Because love is patient, kind, being yourself, forgiving, delighting, sharing dreams, and rejoicing with family, friends and other people. Love without God is jealous, boasting, arrogant, rude, resentful and irritable. The real meaning of the word love is impossible to comprehend or understand if you don't know who God is, because God Is Love.

Sometimes negative thoughts and ideas come up now and then to show me where I still need improvement.

"One Day At A Time Sweet Jesus. That's All I Am Asking From You", that is my daily song when I feel like my back is against the wall, and I don't have anyone to be there for me. In spite, of how I feel at times, I still remain faithful to Him, hoping to rejoice with Him at His coming. I just need to give myself to God daily without reservation and He will work wonders in my life.

> *"God cares about everything, even the smallest details of our lives. The promise of the Lord is certain. He blesses those who trust in Him and pray supplications to Him."*

Thank you dear Lord, for keeping me day by day. Some days it's such a struggle. But in spite of the struggle, I am not giving up on You. Sometimes I am not worthy to call your name, but in spite of my sinfulness, You are my creator. So I come to you for guidance and protection. Father God, day by day I pray for those who have hatred and animosity against me. Touch their heart and give them a clean mind.

Sometimes, I wonder why we go to church if our heart is so evil and dirty. Why read the bible if we do not forgive or have compassion? What God are we praising? I know my weaknesses and I am asking everyone I associate with to pray for my weaknesses: my mouth, my lip, my tongue.

Each day, I pray to be cleansed of my sins, but at times I feel the sins of my past still follow me. Often, I will tell my family, friends, and others how much I love them and appreciate them, but the feeling isn't reciprocated. Thank God that I do not give in to the negative responses anymore. Thank God for the joy in my life and my joy in Christ that keeps me from succumbing to anger and sadness. I can let go of animosity. I will not let anyone put me down and keep me down because of my past.

Chapter 6:
Closing Words

"Father God, forgive me when I allow anger to overcome me when things don't go the way I'd like them. Help me to trust that you are with me through all situations and that you have a plan for things to turn out for my good.

Father God, I just want to thank you for the little wisdom you grant to me so that I can share my thoughts. Thank you for your continual guidance. I give my worries to you. Sometimes the journey is so rough and rugged with trials, temptations and pain. Father God, I know you love me, and you know my problems, so I am surrendering them to you.

Father God, please allow your spirit to enter into the homes of my family and friends and my associates. Let us all put aside our animosity and come together as one family. That is my prayer to you in Jesus's name, Amen."

I hope when reading this, you have an open mind to receive what I must say. Previously, I had written a couple of booklets which received a lot of comments and concerns, both positive and negative from friends and family. Nevertheless, the feedback that I received has not deterred me from my purpose in writing. I have always wanted to write a book about my childhood and these comments have fueled me to keep going, so I thank you.

In spite of my personal struggles, I thank the Lord for allowing me to live. Living life is a blessing. What is life? For me, life is an opportunity, so I take it as it comes. The journey that comes, I complete it. The challenges that I meet, I overcome them. The duties I have, I perform them. The promises I made, I fulfilled them. The tragedies that came, I faced them. I'm glad I achieved these goals. Glad am I that I lived for that blessing. To see the sunrise and to see the sunset. To see the trees grow and to see the flowers bloom. To see God's creation with all the different animals. Happy that he saved my life to be a wife, to be a mother, to see my children grow up. To have friends and family.

My Family

I thank God for providing a loving husband and a good father to my children. He did not come short of bringing joy, peace, and happiness to my family and me. I must emphasize that my husband has been a loving husband, a great father-figure, a family-oriented person and a provider for the family, no matter how small it is. He is liked by my family so much that you would think that I was the in-law. He supported me in my journey to obtaining my GED. At my first attempt, I failed and was discouraged, but he never stopped encouraging me to keep trying until I passed even though it took more than one try. Anything I set out to accomplish in hopes of bettering myself, he has supported 100%. He is more than just a husband, but also my best friend, my confidant, and my everything.

To my husband: I love you with all my heart. You are a rainbow of joy which adds color to my life. I want you to know that I cherish you. I think that we are a couple that God has joined together and no man can put asunder. Yes, we do have our ups and downs, but which couple doesn't? I thank you for sharing your life with me, and always being there throughout the years. With the guidance of God, we will continue to have many more years to sing together, cry together, and dance together.

To my first born: I just want you to know that I love you with all my heart and I am proud of you. The fact that you were able to persevere through life's challenges and chose to continue your education, has made me a proud and happy mom. Keep it up, and remember that the sky is the limit. Believe in yourself and you can achieve great heights in life, but remember to put your faith in God first. I can see what an amazing woman you have become and a great mother to your daughter. I hope you have embedded in my grand-daughter the importance of education like I have done with you. Whatever circumstances come your way, please do not let it separate you from her. I pray that you will live an outstanding life so that my grand-daughter can follow in your footsteps. Never give up on your journey.

To my second born: I love you with all my heart. I am proud of you and your positive outlook on life. I am happy to see the effort you are making to pursue your degree and manage your job at the same time. Keep it up and continue to do well. Continue to follow in God's footsteps and never walk away from your faith. I love you always, and the entire family loves you, too. I wish for you the best that life offers. Make a difference, and let your light shine wherever you go. I wish you the best and always remember, put God first in your life.

We invite you to view the complete
selection of titles we publish at:
www.ASPECTBooks.com

We encourage you to write us
with your thoughts about this,
or any other book we publish at:
info@ASPECTBooks.com

ASPECT Books' titles may be purchased in
bulk quantities for educational, fund-raising,
business, or promotional use.
bulksales@ASPECTBooks.com

Finally, if you are interested in seeing
your own book in print, please contact us at:
publishing@ASPECTBooks.com

We are happy to review your manuscript at no charge.

www.ingramcontent.com/pod-product-compliance
Lightning Source LLC
Chambersburg PA
CBHW070559160426
43199CB00014B/2550